Her Majesty's

TOWER OF LONDON

ABOVE: *The mighty White Tower, seen from the south bank of the Thames. William the Conqueror created his fortress on a site where 1,000 years earlier Claudius, a previous conqueror, had built a fort. The Tower of London still dominates the river approaches to the city.*

The TOWER OF LONDON

A Brief History by Colonel Sir Thomas Butler Bt

The Tower of London has been called 'The Cradle of the English race'. It is well named for it was here that England had her first beginnings as a nation. It is, moreover, the oldest palace, fortress and prison in Europe.

The great fortress was created by William the Conqueror, nearly 900 years ago. The site he chose was the one on which Claudius, the Roman Emperor, had built a fort more than a thousand years earlier: traces of the Roman wall can still be seen in the Tower. It was well chosen for two main reasons; firstly the fortress commanded the river approaches to the city and secondly, it protected the king and government from those citizens of London who did not take kindly to their Norman overlords.

At first the stronghold probably consisted of timber buildings defended by a palisade of stakes, but in 1078 William I commissioned Gundulf, a monk from Normandy, to build a great tower or keep. The work took twenty years and much of the stone used came from Caen in Normandy.

As king succeeded king, the fortress was enlarged by building walls and smaller towers around the central keep. Towards the end of the 12th century, Richard I added to its might by encircling it with a moat fed by the River Thames.

As will be seen from the plan, the Tower of London is roughly square in shape with two lines of defensive walls enclosing Gundulf's great tower which for centuries has been known as the White Tower. At intervals on the inner wall are thirteen smaller towers. This is the Inner Ward, the only surviving original entrance being on the south side under the Bloody Tower. The outer wall is defended by six towers on the river face and by two semicircular bastions at the north-east and north-west.

Over the centuries the Tower has served many purposes. It has been a citadel; a royal palace; a prison for dangerous offenders against the State; the only place of coinage for all England; an armoury for warlike supplies; the treasury of the regalia and Crown Jewels; the record office of the king's Courts of Justice; a royal menagerie and the first royal observatory.

The mint, the menagerie, the observatory and the record office have long since moved elsewhere, but the Tower is still a garrisoned fortress and technically a royal palace. The last sovereign to reside there, however, was James I.

The Tower of London has always been controlled directly by the Sovereign and commanded by a Constable appointed by the Crown. The first Constable was Geoffrey de Mandeville, a Norman knight. Prelates and politicians have also held the post, but since the late 18th century distinguished soldiers have been appointed. The Constable, who has direct access to the Sovereign, no longer resides in the Tower but entrusts the day-to-day administration to a Resident Governor who lives in the Queen's House, and to two deputy governors. The Department of the Environment is responsible for the maintenance of the Tower.

The Living Tower Today

So many great historical places are today lifeless monuments of the past. Those who administer the Tower of London like to think of it as a living place which indeed it is. Within its bounds is a community of some three hundred men, women and children. It has its own social club, restaurant, tennis court and playground; its own chaplain and two chapels; its own doctor, carpenters, plumbers, stonemasons, electricians and of course its guardians—the Yeomen Warders.

The Entrance

Most visitors to the Tower will pass over Tower Hill. On the brow, within the railings of Trinity Square, once stood a permanent scaffold. This was set up in 1465, but the earliest execution recorded was that of Simon of Sudbury, Archbishop of Canterbury, who was beheaded in 1381 by Wat Tyler's supporters. Over one hundred enemies of the State died on this spot, the last being Simon Fraser, Lord Lovat, in 1747, for his part in the second Jacobite rebellion.

The Tower is entered at the foot of Tower Hill near where used to stand the Bulwark Gate. It was here that prisoners for execution were handed over to the Sheriff of London. Just within the gate is the Tower restaurant standing on the site of the old Lion Tower.

★

FACING PAGE: *The Tower of London from the Thames, an aquatint by William Daniell, 1804. The dome of St. Paul's Cathedral and the spires of many of the City churches are visible in the background.*

RIGHT: *The Middle Tower, built in the time of Edward I, but largely reconstructed in the early 18th century when windows were put in and the walls refaced.*

The Lion Tower

In this wide semicircular tower the royal menagerie was housed. Henry I kept lions in the tower and in 1235 Henry II was sent three leopards by Frederick II. In 1252 he received a white bear from the king of Norway and two years later an elephant from Louis of France. James I is said to have entertained his guests to a bear-baiting display in the Bear Pit. In 1834 the menagerie was sent to Regent's Park where it formed the nucleus of the present London Zoo. The tower was then demolished.

The Middle Tower

A short causeway leads to the Middle Tower, built in the late 13th century, but largely rebuilt in the early 18th century. The royal coat of arms of George I is seen above the archway. This archway, together with those of Byward Tower and the Bloody Tower, were defended by portcullises, two of which remain. Beyond the Middle Tower is the moat which is crossed by another causeway where there was once a third drawbridge.

The Byward Tower

The Byward Tower probably derives its name from By-the-ward and gives access to the Outer Ward. It is here that the password is still demanded by the sentry at night. On either side of the archway are guardrooms with vaulted roofs and hooded fireplaces. A 14th-century wall paint-

Continued on page 4

3

ing, of St John the Baptist and St Michael against a background of leopards of England and fleurs-de-lis of France, was uncovered in 1953.

The Outer Ward

The Byward Tower archway leads to the Outer Ward. Ahead is Water Lane, once ten feet lower than it is today. Immediately on the left is Mint Street. Here too are the casemates where many of the Yeoman Warders live, and at one time there was a tavern with a golden chain as its sign on the site of No. 1 Casemate.

The Bell Tower

This stands on the south-west corner of the Inner Ward. It was built in the early 13th century and is so called because of the belfry on top. In the past, when the bell was rung in alarm, drawbridges were raised, portcullises dropped and gates shut. The bell is still rung in the evening to warn the visitors on the wharf that it is time to leave.

The Bell Tower has only two cells and no connecting staircase. At its base there is ten feet of solid masonry and the walls are eight feet thick. In the 16th century the Queen's House, then called the Lieutenant's Lodgings, was connected to it.

Among the many prisoners confined in the Bell Tower were Sir Thomas More, the Lord Chancellor and John Fisher, Bishop of Rochester. They were imprisoned in 1534 for refusing to accept the Act of Succession and to acknowledge Henry VIII as supreme head of the Church. They were executed within a month of each other and both were canonised. Their bodies rest in the Chapel of St Peter ad Vincula.

Princess Elizabeth, later Elizabeth I, was also imprisoned in the Bell Tower. She was sent there by her half-sister Mary I in 1554. The princess was allowed to exercise on the battlements (thereafter known as Elizabeth's Walk) and to take her meals in the Lieutenant's Lodgings.

Her health suffered and as no charges could be proved against her she was released after six weeks. Four years later she became Queen.

St Thomas's Tower and Traitors' Gate

Farther along Water Lane on the right is St Thomas's Tower standing above Traitors' Gate. In about 1230 Henry III had a channel cut through the wharf and outer wall to enable the royal barge to enter the Tower from the Thames and set down passengers at the royal apartments in the Wakefield Tower. As the channel weakened the riverside defences of the fortress it was protected by a massive gate and portcullis. This was first called Water Gate, but later, when it was used for landing the Crown's enemies, it became known as Traitors' Gate. All important prisoners entered the Tower through this gate. According to legend when Princess Elizabeth arrived on Palm Sunday 1554 she refused at first to land at the gate, angrily proclaiming that she was no traitor. A sharp shower of rain, however, caused her to change her mind. Later when as queen she visited the Tower she insisted on passing through Traitors' Gate. 'What was good enough for Elizabeth the Princess is good enough for Elizabeth the Queen,' she is supposed to have told the Constable.

To strengthen further the southern defences Henry III built a tower above the gate and named it after St Thomas Becket who had been Constable in 1162. In 1610 a romantic escape was made from St Thomas's Tower by William Seymour, a grandson of Lady Catherine Grey and afterwards second Duke of Somerset. He had been imprisoned by James I for secretly marrying Arabella Stuart who was the immediate heir to the Throne. Seymour had noticed that a carter was allowed into the Tower daily to sell hay and faggots. The carter was bribed and at an agreed place stopped the cart. The prisoner, disguised in a smock and wig, stepped out and took the reins, and whilst the carter hid in the hay the cart was successfully driven out of the Tower. Unhappily Seymour's plan to rejoin his wife miscarried. Arabella Stuart was herself sent to the Tower in 1611 where she died insane four years later.

Continued on page 6

FACING PAGE: *The Byward Tower was built at the end of the 13th century, although the top storey is largely of 18th and 19th-century origin. It probably derives its name from 'By-the-Ward', though some say that the name came from the fact that from earliest times a byword or password must be given at night before passing through the gate. This custom is still in force today.*

ABOVE: *The Bell Tower is one of the oldest towers. It was constructed during the late 12th and early 13th centuries. Its name comes from the belfry on the top. From the middle of the 16th century it was used as a prison for more important people—Sir Thomas More, 1534–5; John Fisher, Bishop of Rochester 1535 and Princess (later Queen) Elizabeth, who was brought here through Traitors' Gate on Palm Sunday 1554.*

RIGHT: *The Cradle Tower and beyond it the Lanthorn Tower. The Cradle Tower was built in the 14th century. It has an entrance from the moat and was once used as a water-gate to the Royal Apartments.*

The Yeomen Warders

The history of the Yeomen Warders is as ancient as that of the fortress itself. They are the custodians of the Tower and of the Crown Jewels.

At one time Yeomen Warders were able to purchase warden-ships for about £309. In Tudor times especially the appointment was highly prized because wealthy prisoners were all too ready to pay for privileged treatment. If a Yeoman Warder died on duty his money remained with the Constable, but retiring Warders could sell their posts to suitable candidates. Hence the toast drunk when a new warder is installed: 'May he never die a Yeoman Warder'.

The practice of purchase was abolished by the Duke of Wellington when he was Constable. The duke also ruled that Yeomen Warders were to be recruited from soldiers who had held the rank of sergeant or above. His rule has been modified in recent times. Now all applicants must have served as warrant officers or colour sergeants in the Army, Royal Marines, or the Royal Air Force, and they must also hold the Long Service and Good Conduct medal.

Yeomen Warders are usually seen at the Tower in the blue undress uniform granted to them by Queen Victoria in 1858. Their gorgeous scarlet and gold dress which they have been allowed, on the authority of Edward VI, to wear on state occasions since 1552, is similar in design to the dress worn by Henry VII's bodyguard. The Chief Warder carries a Staff surmounted by a silver model of the White Tower, and his second-in-command, the Yeoman Gaoler, a ceremonial axe. The Yeoman Warders are armed with a halberd or pike known as a partisan.

The Yeomen Warders at the Tower should not be confused with the Yeomen of the Guard. The latter is a part-time force responsible for the safety of the Sovereign on state occasions. They wear the same resplendent ceremonial dress as the Yeomen Warders with the addition of a cross-belt over the left shoulder.

The Wakefield Tower

Opposite Traitors' Gate is the Wakefield Tower which was built in the early 13th century. Here the Crown Jewels were housed from 1870 until 1967 when they were removed to a specially constructed chamber in the Waterloo Block. The tower is probably named after William de Wakefield, King's Clerk and holder of the custody of the Exchanges in 1334.

Continued on page 8

★

ABOVE: *The Resident Governor about to inspect the Yeomen Warders on parade for the Easter Monday service in the Chapel of St Peter ad Vincula.*

FACING PAGE: *The Chief Warder* (left) *and the Yeoman Gaoler.*

By a curious coincidence prisoners from the Battle of Wakefield were held there in 1460.

In the 14th century the State records were transferred to the Wakefield Tower from the White Tower and in surveys of the period the building is referred to as the Record Tower.

The tower has two chambers, the ground floor acting as a guardroom to the postern which led to the royal apartments above. These apartments were destroyed by Cromwell. The upper floor now contains a large and magnificent octagonal vaulted chamber in which there is an oratory. On a white marble tablet let into the oratory floor is the inscription: 'By tradition Henry VI died here May 21st 1471'. Henry VI who was the founder of Eton College and of King's College, Cambridge, is supposed to have been murdered on the orders of the Duke of Gloucester, later Richard III. On the anniversary of his death, a touching little ceremony takes place at 6 p.m. A representative of Eton places three white lilies tied in the Eton colours of light blue on the tablet and one from King's College offers a sheaf of white roses bound with the purple ribbon of the college.

The Bloody Tower

The gateway of the Bloody Tower leads into the Inner Ward. The gateway was built by Henry III and the tower was added by Richard II. Originally called the Garden Tower, it gained its present name in the 16th century because of the murderous deeds which took place in its dark rooms. One such deed was the killing of the princes, Edward V and his younger brother Richard, Duke of York. This occurred in 1483 supposedly on the orders of the Duke of Gloucester, afterwards Richard III, but there are some who strongly oppose this view, and name Henry Tudor, later Henry VII, as the culprit. The generally accepted version of the murder is that Elizabeth Woodville, widow of Edward IV, was forced to allow her sons to live in the Tower, ostensibly to enable the 13-year-old king to prepare for his coronation.

The then Constable, Sir Robert Brackenbury, was asked to take part in the murder but refused to help. Thereupon Sir James Tyrell was sent to the Tower with orders to force the Constable to surrender his keys for one night. Sir James's agents found the two boys asleep. One was suffocated with a pillow whilst the other boy was stabbed to death. The murderers carried the bodies down a narrow, winding staircase and buried them under a covering of rubble in the basement. When the Constable returned he was horrified to learn what had happened and ordered the priest to give the princes a Christian burial. They were reburied close to the White Tower but all knowledge of the grave was lost for Sir Robert Brackenbury was killed at the battle of Bosworth and the priest disappeared.

In 1674, during the reign of Charles II, skeletons of two boys were unearthed near the White Tower and in the belief that the grave of the princes had been found the king ordered that the bodies be moved to Westminster Abbey. The bones were exhumed in 1933 when a royal com-

mission examined them. In the opinion of the experts the remains were undoubtedly those of the princes, but controversy still clouds the tragedy.

Many other tragic figures of history suffered imprisonment or death in the Bloody Tower. Archbishop Cranmer and Bishops Ridley and Latimer who were condemned to death for heresy in 1555, were imprisoned in the tower before being burned at the stake at Oxford; Henry Percy, Earl of Northumberland, died there in mysterious circumstances in 1585; Sir Thomas Overbury, poet and courtier, was a victim of Court intrigue: his food was poisoned and he is supposed to have swallowed enough poison to kill twenty men before he died in 1613. Another prisoner in the Bloody Tower was the notorious Judge Jeffreys. He also died there but his death in 1689 was caused by disease.

Sir Walter Raleigh spent most of his thirteen years' imprisonment in the Bloody Tower, but he was able to perform many scientific experiments. He is credited with having discovered a method of distilling fresh water from salt water. Also during his imprisonment he wrote his vast *History of the World* which was published in 1614, four years before he was beheaded at Westminster. An early copy of this is on view in the Bloody Tower.

The White Tower

The great central keep is 90 feet high and is of massive construction, the walls varying from 15 feet thickness at the base to almost 11 feet in the upper part. Above the battlements rise four turrets; three of them are square, but that on the north-east is circular. This turret once contained the first royal observatory.

The original single entrance was on the south side and it was reached by an external staircase. There were no doors at ground level. The walls on the upper floors were penetrated by narrow slits positioned in wide splays. On the southern side, four pairs of the original double slits remain. In the late 17th and early 18th centuries all others were replaced by Sir Christopher Wren with the windows seen today. There is a well in the basement which is probably Roman.

In the White Tower the medieval kings of England lived with their families and their court. Here was the seat of government and here the laws of the land were made. The royal family lived on the top storey; the council chamber was on the floor below. In this chamber in 1399 Richard II was forced to sign away his throne, and in 1483 Richard III summarily sentenced Lord Hastings to death.

On the first floor is the exquisite chapel of St John the Evangelist where

Continued on page 10

★

FACING PAGE: *St Thomas's Tower seen from Tower Wharf. Beneath the tower is Traitors' Gate.*

ABOVE: *The grim portal of Traitors' Gate through which all supposed traitors to the Crown passed on their way to the dungeons. The massive iron and oaken gates were also opened to allow barges to enter the Tower.*

the royal family and the court worshipped and where new knights of the Order of the Bath spent their vigil the night before a coronation. It is one of the most perfect specimens of Norman architecture in this country.

To this historic chapel the remains of Henry VI were carried after his murder in the Wakefield Tower in 1471. In 1503 the body of Queen Elizabeth, known as the 'White Rose of York', the wife of Henry VII, lay in state surrounded by 800 lighted candles. Queen Mary Tudor was married in the chapel by proxy to King Philip of Spain, and in this same chapel poor Lady Jane Grey, uncrowned queen of nine days, knelt before the altar and prayed on the eve of her execution.

Few prisoners have succeeded in escaping from the White Tower. One successful escape was made in 1101 by Ralph de Flambard, an affluent and much-hated tax-gatherer in the reign of Henry I. A prisoner with money at that time could buy everything he wanted except his freedom (he could even do that on occasion) and Flambard won over his guards by inviting them to his parties. On the night of his escape he gave a banquet to which he invited not only all the warders and soldiers in the tower but the company of knights responsible for guarding him. His friends outside the Tower bribed the guards on the outer gates. Wine was lavishly served from huge jars and as the evening progressed everyone except Flambard became very drunk. A coil of rope was hidden in one of the jars and with this he began his descent from the tall tower. Unhappily for Flambard the rope was too short and he found himself hanging in mid-air. Eventually his arms gave way and he plummeted to the ground. His friends found him bruised and battered and carried him to a boat on the river. He reached France and

later became Bishop of Durham.

Two hundred years later, Gruffyd, a native Welsh prince, attempted a similar escape from the White Tower and was killed when the rope snapped.

The White Tower now contains one of the finest collections of arms and armour in the world. (See page 24.)

The Beauchamp Tower

This semicircular tower was built in the reign of Henry III and probably owes its name to Thomas Beauchamp, Earl of Warwick, who was confined there by Richard II in 1393. Of especial interest are the inscriptions carved on the stone walls by prisoners. The most elaborate is a memorial to the five brothers Dudley, one of whom was Lord Guildford Dudley, husband of Lady Jane Grey. This unhappy pair were executed in 1554. The Governor of the Tower was allowed 6s. 8d. per day for food for each brother during their imprisonment.

The Queen's House

The house was built about 1530 possibly for Queen Anne Boleyn, but she lived there only as a prisoner for eighteen days awaiting her execution. It is a very fine example of half-timbered Tudor architecture. Within a few years of completion, a floor was inserted at second-storey level in the lofty hall making what is known as the Council Chamber. This was frequently used by Mary I and James I. The chamber has a magnificent 16th-century rafted ceiling and contains an elaborate tablet commemorating the Gunpowder Plot erected in 1608 by the then Governor, Sir William Waad. In this room Guy Fawkes was interrogated and, after torture on the rack in the White Tower, signed a confession incriminating his fellow conspirators.

Adjoining the Council Chambers is a room from which Lord Nithsdale, a Jacobite rebel, escaped disguised as a woman on the eve of his execution in 1716. William Penn, the famous Quaker who founded the State of Pennsylvania in America, was also a prisoner in this house.

Until the late 19th century the house was known as the Lieutenant's Lodgings. Queen Victoria then decided that it was to be called The Queen's House. On the accession of Edward VII it became the King's House and so it remained until Queen Elizabeth II came to the throne. It is the residence of the Governor of the Tower and is not open to the public.

Continued on page 14

★

FACING PAGE (left): *It is grimly appropriate that the only axe now in the Tower of London is to be seen in the Bloody Tower. It was used for the execution of Simon, Lord Lovat on Tower Hill in 1747.*

FACING PAGE (right): *The narrow stairway in the Bloody Tower down which the bodies of the little princes were probably carried.*

ABOVE: *The Bloody Tower and gateway and the circular Wakefield Tower.*

RIGHT: *The marble tablet in the oratory of the Wakefield Tower marking the place where, by tradition, Henry VI fell when he was murdered in 1471.*

The starkly beautiful early Norman chapel of St John the Evangelist in the great White Tower which is seen on the facing page.

The Crown Jewels

The Crown Jewels are housed in the underground Jewel House beneath the Waterloo Barracks. The incomparable collection of crowns, sceptres, orbs, swords and other regalia and gold and silver plate is displayed in a specially designed modern setting. On this page are seen the Imperial State Crown, the Sceptre with the Cross, and (right) Queen Elizabeth the Queen Mother's crown.

In the Imperial State Crown are set jewels of great antiquity and historical significance. The oldest is Edward the Confessor's sapphire, believed to have been worn by him in a ring and now mounted in the *cross patee* above the monde. The great gem above the rim is the ancient balas-ruby known as the Black Prince's ruby, which is said to have been given to him by Pedro the Cruel of Castile.

From the intersection of the arches hang four superb drop pearls, the so-called Queen Elizabeth's Ear-rings, but there is no evidence that she ever wore them in this way. Set in the rim at the back of the crown is the Stuart sapphire. It is probably much older than its name implies, but is known to have been in the possession of James II when he fled to France after his deposition. It was formerly mounted in the rim at the front, but was displaced by the second Star of Africa, cut from the Cullinan diamond. In addition to these jewels, the Imperial State Crown contains over 3,000 diamonds and pearls, as well as fine sapphires, emeralds and rubies.

The Royal Sceptre with the Cross is a rod of chased gold, with the peerless Star of Africa cut from the Cullinan diamond held in a heart-shaped mount. Above this is a superb amethyst and the sceptre is surmounted with a diamond-encrusted cross set with an emerald.

Queen Elizabeth the Queen Mother's Crown was made for her coronation as queen consort in 1937. This graceful crown is set with diamonds, dominated by the famous Koh-i-noor. Its Indian name means 'Mountain of Light' and the jewel has a long and turbulent history. Tradition says that its male owners will suffer misfortune, but women who possess it will rule the world.

★

Note: *The Crown Jewels and Coronation Ritual* is a companion volume published in the Pride of Britain series. The author, Sir Thomas Butler, describes in detail the regalia and its significance and use in the coronation ceremony.

In the White Tower and new Armouries (above) is the National Collection of Arms and Armour. A description of the collection will be found on page 24.

ABOVE RIGHT: *Armour of Charles I. Possibly made in England c. 1625, it is richly engraved and gilded.*

RIGHT: *A magnificent pair of silver mounted flintlock pistols with the crest of the Dukes of Marlborough.*

FACING PAGE: *Part of the Crown Jewels collection: The Imperial State Crown, made for Queen Victoria's coronation in 1838; Queen Elizabeth The Queen Mother's Crown, made for her coronation in 1937, and the Royal Sceptre with the Cross which contains the largest cut diamond in the world, the Star of Africa.*
(Photograph Crown Copyright. Reproduced with the permission of the Controller of Her Majesty's Stationery Office.)

15

Tower Green

On the west side of the White Tower is Tower Green bounded on the north by the Chapel of St Peter ad Vincula and on the south side by the Queen's House. On the west of the Green stands the Beauchamp Tower.

The Scaffold Site

Between the Chapel and Tower Green is a small paved area. A scaffold was erected here for the beheading of those whose public execution on Tower Hill might have incited the people to riot. The names of the six tragic figures who died on this fateful spot are inscribed on a board. They include three queens of England, Anne Boleyn, Katherine Howard and Lady Jane Grey; a one-time governess to Mary I, Margaret, Countess of Salisbury; a lady-in-waiting to Queen Anne, Jane, Viscountess Rochford; and Elizabeth I's favourite and supposed suitor, Robert Devereux, Earl of Essex. Anne Boleyn pleaded for a sword to be used instead of axe and was despatched by an expert executioner summoned from Calais. In contrast to this swift execution was the bloody hewing down of Margaret, Countess of Salisbury, who refused to lay her head on the block. According to legend, Essex to the last moment expected to be reprieved. Years earlier, Elizabeth had given him a ring and made him promise that he would return the ring if he ever needed her help. This he did on the eve of his execution, but the lady-in-waiting who was to give it to the Queen kept it until after his death. Elizabeth is supposed to have turned on her with: 'God may forgive you but I never can'.

In 1483 Lord Hastings was beheaded nearby after a quarrel with Richard III during which he accused him of causing the deaths of Henry VI and the Duke of Clarence. In his fury the king is said to have ordered his guards to deal with Lord Hastings at once exclaiming, 'I shall not dine until your head is off!'

Continued on page 19

★

ABOVE: *The White Tower, built in the 11th century. On the right can be seen a fragment of the Roman wall, which once enclosed the square mile of the city of London.*

HENRY VI: *He was pious but disastrously weak, and was twice deposed and committed to the Tower, where he was finally murdered.*

SIR THOMAS MORE: *A friend of Henry VIII, but he refused to acknowledge the validity of the king's divorce from Queen Catherine of Aragon.*

ANNE BOLEYN: *Second queen of Henry VIII and mother of Elizabeth I, she was beheaded on Tower green by a French executioner for alleged infidelity.*

LADY JANE GREY: *The queen of nine days. She was executed in 1554.*

ARCHBISHOP LAUD: *A fervent supporter of Charles I, he was beheaded in 1645.*

PRINCESS ELIZABETH: *Confined by Mary I in the Bell Tower, 1554.*

SAMUEL PEPYS: *Accused of conspiracy in the Popish Plot; later released.*

SIR WALTER RALEIGH: *Imprisoned for twelve years and beheaded in 1618.*

LORD LOVAT: *In 1747 the last person to be executed in the Tower of London.*

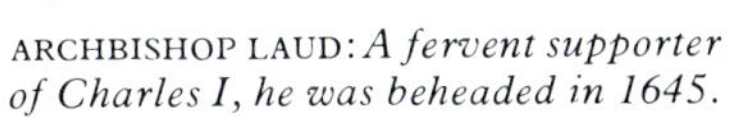

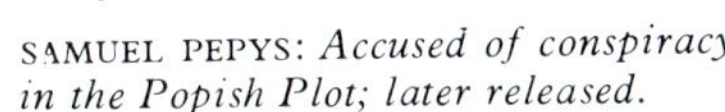

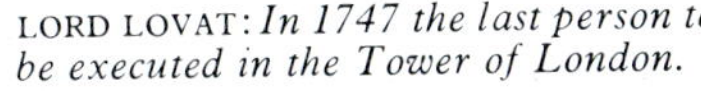

ABOVE: *The Queen's House on Tower Green. Next to it is the Yeoman Gaoler's House, where from a window Lady Jane Grey watched her husband leave his prison in the nearby Beauchamp Tower for his execution. She later saw his headless body being carried to the Chapel of St Peter. From the same window she watched the scaffold for her own execution being erected.*

LEFT: *The Council Chamber in the Queen's House. In this room conspirators of the Gunpowder Plot were interrogated.*

FACING PAGE (left): *The changing of the guard outside the Queen's House.*

FACING PAGE (right): *The cell in the Queen's House in which Sir Thomas More was imprisoned by Henry VIII. He was executed in July 1535 and was buried in St Peter's Chapel.*

18

The Chapel Royal of St Peter ad Vincula (St Peter in Chains)

This historic chapel is the oldest chapel royal in England. The first building was erected in the early 12th century and rebuilt some hundred years later. In 1512 it was damaged by fire and much of the present structure dates from Henry VIII's time. The existing north wall was probably the south wall of the earlier chapel. When the Tower was a royal residence the chapel was used mainly by the soldiers, Yeomen Warders and prisoners, but it was also a place where the sovereign worshipped in public although normally the royal family would use the private chapel of St John in the White Tower.

In this little chapel most of those who died on Tower Hill and six of the seven executed on Tower Green were laid to rest under flagstones without ceremony. Among them are three queens of England and four dukes. The historian Stow, writing at the time of Elizabeth I, put it succinctly: 'Two dukes between two queens, to wit, the Duke of Somerset and the Duke of Northumberland, between Queen Anne and Queen Katherine, all four Beheaded'. Nearly three centuries later Macaulay described the Chapel of St Peter thus: 'In truth there is no sadder spot on earth'. Today although its historic and tragic past is not forgotten the chapel has happier associations. It is a live place of worship where every Sunday morning glorious music and singing can be heard. The choir has become justly celebrated under the direction of its Master of Music who plays the organ built by Dr Bernard Schmidt in 1678 for the Old Palace of Whitehall.

The Martin Tower

Built by Henry III, this tower is famous as the scene of Colonel Thomas Blood's fruitless attempt to steal the Crown Jewels. After the Restoration, the newly-made regalia was kept in the Martin Tower in the sole custody of the Deputy Keeper of the Jewels, a man named Talbot Edwards who lived with his family in the tower.

Blood, disguised as a clergyman, became very friendly with Edwards, even to the point of proposing a marriage between the old man's daughter and a supposed nephew of his. Early on a May morning in 1671, the colonel appeared by appointment with his 'nephew' and a friend to arrange the marriage. Whilst awaiting the ladies, Blood suggested that his friends might see the Crown Jewels. As soon as the chamber was opened Edwards was

Continued on page 20

attacked and badly injured. Blood hid the State Crown beneath his cloak, one accomplice slipped the orb into his breeches, while the other began filing the sceptre in half to make it more portable. They were then unexpectedly disturbed by Edward's son returning from abroad and a running fight followed during which all three were captured.

Blood eventually obtained an audience with Charles II to whom he remarked that 'it was a gallant attempt'. Charles—with strange leniency—immediately pardoned Blood, granted him a pension and promised that his Irish estates, seized at the Restoration, would be restored.

Edwards was granted £200 by the Exchequer and his son was given £100. The old man, however, was forced to sell his expectations for half its value, and he died of his injuries soon afterwards.

The Salt Tower

This tower, built by Henry III about 1235, was used in later days as a prison for Jesuits. It contains a number of interesting inscriptions, the most notable being a complicated diagram cut in stone for casting horoscopes. The inscription records that 'Hew Draper of Brystow made this spheer the 30 daye of Maye anno 1561'. Draper was imprisoned for attempted witchcraft in 1561.

In several places on the walls a pierced heart, hand and foot have been carved. This symbol signifies the wounds of Christ. As in other towers where Jesuits were imprisoned, the monogram I.H.S. with a cross above the 'H' occurs in several places. This sign was used by members of the Society of Jesus.

The Ceremony of the Keys

The Ceremony of the Keys is the traditional locking up of the Tower by night. It is one of the oldest and most colourful ceremonies of its kind, having taken place for the last 700 years in much the same form as it is seen today.

Every night at exactly seven minutes to 10 o'clock the Chief Warder emerges from the Byward Tower wearing his long red coat and Tudor bonnet, carrying in one hand a candle lantern and in the other hand The Queen's Keys. With solemn tread he moves along Water Lane, to Traitors' Gate where his escort provided by one of the regiments of Foot Guards awaits him. He hands the lantern to an escorting soldier and the party then moves to the outer gate. En route all guards and sentries salute The Queen's Keys. After locking the outer gate the Chief Warder and escort retrace their steps. The great oak gates of the Middle and Byward Towers are locked in turn. They now return along Water Lane towards Traitors' Gate where in the shadows of the Bloody Tower archway a sentry waits. When the party approaches the sentry challenges: 'Halt! Who goes there?' The Chief Warder answers: 'The Keys'. 'Whose keys?' the sentry demands. 'Queen Elizabeth's keys'. 'Pass Queen Elizabeth's keys. All's well' is the sentry's final rejoinder. The party then proceeds through the Bloody Tower archway and up towards the steps where the main guard is drawn up. The Chief Warder and escort halt at the foot of the steps and the officer in charge of the guard gives the command to present arms. The Chief Warder moves two paces forward, raises his Tudor bonnet high in the air and calls: 'God preserve Queen Elizabeth'. The guard answers 'Amen' just as the clock chimes ten and the bugler sounds the Last Post. The Chief Warder takes the keys to the Queen's House and the guard is dismissed.

Royal Salutes

Royal salutes are fired from Tower Wharf. A salute of 62 guns is fired on anniversaries of the birth, accession and coronation of the sovereign. On other occasions salutes of shorter length are fired including one of 41 guns on the birth of a royal infant. Salutes are fired by the Honourable Artillery Company, a famous territor- ial regiment which is one of the oldest in the British Army.

Beating the Bounds

Every third year, on Ascension Day, boys whose families are connected with the Tower 'beat the bounds' of the Tower Liberty. They assemble on Tower Green where they are given white wands. At each boundary mark the Tower Chaplain says: 'Cursed is he who removeth his neighbours' landmark' and the Chief Warder adds: 'Whack it, boys, whack it!' The boys duly obey with great gusto. The custom of beating the bounds dates from Saxon days when boundaries were often marked by stones.

Tower Bridge

Tower Bridge is a source of never-ending fascination to visitors to London. Many who come to the Tower of London often wait a long time hoping to see the roadway raised to allow an ocean-going ship to enter the Pool of London. Although the two bascules which carry the roadway each weigh over 1,000 tons, they can be raised in under two minutes.

The bridge was built between 1886 and 1894 by the City of London Corporation to link the south-eastern suburbs with the city and eastern London. It cost over a million pounds. Nearby is Tower Pier, embarkation point for the river launches which take tourists on short trips to places of interest.

The river foreshore in front of the Tower of London, which is part of the Tower lands, is used as a pleasure beach by children. They have the late Lord Wakefield to thank for this open-air delight. In 1934 when he was Sir Charles Wakefield, he obtained King George V's sanction for the foreshore to be converted to a playground by spreading hundreds of tons of sand on the gravel beach. It was opened that year and has been popular ever since.

FACING PAGE: *The Chapel Royal of St Peter ad Vincula and the paved and railed scaffold site on Tower Green. On the board are inscribed the names of the six tragic figures of history beheaded there. A scaffold was erected only when an execution was pending.*

ABOVE: *The Tower ravens are part of the legend of the Tower. A curious superstition dating from the time of Charles II prophesies that when there are no longer ravens in the Tower both the White Tower and the British Commonwealth will fall.*

FACING PAGE (above): *The Honourable Artillery Company firing a 62-gun salute on Tower Wharf to mark the anniversary of The Queen's official birthday.*

FACING PAGE (below): *The installation on Tower Green of Field Marshal Sir Richard Hull, GCB, DSO, as 152nd Constable of the Tower.*
ABOVE: *The final scene of the Ceremony of the Keys. The nightly ritual of locking up the Tower of London is almost completed and the Chief Warder is seen doffing his Tudor bonnet and crying: 'God preserve Queen Elizabeth'.*

The Arms and Armour

A. R. DUFTY

Master of the Armouries
in H.M. Tower of London

The White Tower and the New Armouries contain the national collection of arms and armour. As the most important fortress in the kingdom, the Tower must have held armour and arms from the time it was first built, but in their present form the Armouries date from the time of Henry VIII. The collection—one of the greatest in the world—illustrates the development of arms and armour from the Middle Ages to 1914.

The White Tower is entered through the *Tournament Room*. When the present alterations are completed the display here will be devoted entirely to armour specially designed for use in this warlike exercise. Examples already in the room include the tilt armour for a German type of joust known as the *Scharfrennen*, in which sharp lances were used, and the splendid 'Brocas' helm. The armour was made about 1490 in Germany for use at the court of the Emperor Maximilian I; the tilt helm was probably made in England in the same period.

In tournaments, mounted men ran different courses against each other, each course requiring armour of a special pattern; men also fought against one another on foot and this required armour of yet another pattern. The Armouries contain three foot-combat armours made for Henry VIII, the first in about 1512 and the second about 1515 when he was slim and active, the third in 1540 when he was forty-nine and very portly. The second is remarkable in that all the plates fit together over flanges, thus enabling his height of six feet one inch to be accurately determined. Another important foot-combat armour is one of twelve made in 1591 as a splendid Christmas gift for Christian I of Saxony from his wife. Unhappily the Elector died in the September before the rich present was delivered.

In the adjacent room the collection of hunting and sporting arms includes crossbows and firearms. Here can be traced the technical advances in firearm mechanisms, from the match lock, the snaphance and the wheel lock to the flintlock. The development of decorative techniques is also evident: craftsmen applied or inlaid precious metals, ivory, bone and even mother-of-pearl to enhance the wood they carved and the metal they chiselled with such consummate skill. The contemporary artistic styles from the 15th to the 19th centuries can thus be seen. An especially interesting exhibit is the elegant silver-decorated sporting gun made in Dundee in 1614. It came from the personal gun-room of Louis XIII of France. Another unique exhibit is the Scottish gun made entirely of engraved brass for Charles I when he was a young man.

Through the Chapel of St John is the *Medieval Room* which is now devoted to the earliest arms and armour in the Tower. The exhibits are mostly of the late 14th and 15th centuries and include a superb Italian visored bascinet with its original neck protection of mail. There is also one of the few Gothic horse armours surviving; it was probably made to the order of Waldemar VI of Anhalt-Zerbst (1450–1508).

In the adjoining *Sixteenth-century Room* are shown fine arms and armour dating from that century, but excluding our English products. Most conspicuous is the massive suit of German armour made in about 1540 for a man nearly seven feet tall. Of the middle of the century is the splendid 'Lion' armour embossed with lions' masks and damascened in gold.

On the top floor, the *Tudor Room* is devoted mainly to the armours made in the royal workshops at Greenwich which Henry VIII established about 1514. They include four armours made for the king himself, one engraved and silver-plated, and others made at Greenwich for Tudor courtiers. There is an armour made for one of Elizabeth I's favourites, Robert Dudley, Earl of Leicester, another for William Somerset, Earl of Worcester, another for Sir John Smythe, who vainly championed the use of the long bow many years after its inevitable supersession by firearms.

In the adjoining *Stuart Room* are beautiful little armours made in France or England for the Stuart kings and princes and the London-made harquebus armour of James II. They are the focus of a display devoted to the 17th century, the last period before the disuse of armour.

Separate displays are devoted to the armour, arms and accoutrements of the richly equipped bodyguards, the light and heavy cavalry, and the infantry. The armour of the pikemen was the last to be worn by foot soldiers before the increased efficiency of firearms made its use impractical.

In the basement is the *Mortar Room*, where the bronze mortars on view include one of nine bores used for fireworks at the peace of Aix-la-Chapelle in 1748. At the far end of the room is the entrance to the sub-crypt of the Chapel of St John, where a carved and gilt figure of the Lion of St Mark, a trophy from Corfu, is flanked by a number of the finest small cannon from the Armouries collection. In the adjacent *Cannon Room* the walls are hung with relics of Henry VIII's army and a great array of armour and weapons returned to the Tower after the Civil War. Here also is the greater part of the Armouries collection of cannon, including several from the ships of Henry VIII's navy.

The New Armouries comprise a 17th-century red brick building close to the White Tower. On the ground floor is a representative collection of armour and arms of Africa and the Orient. It is dominated by an armour for an elephant, probably captured at the battle of Plassey in 1757. One Japanese armour on view was presented to James I by the governor of Edo in 1613.

Many of the later sporting firearms on the first floor are of the highest quality. The flintlock guns include one with a silver barrel given by Louis XIV to the first Duke of Richmond, another was sent by Napoleon to Charles IV of Spain, and a third, with matching powder-flask, pair of pistols and stirrups, was made to the order of Elizabeth, Empress of Russia. Here also are the Reverend Alexander Forsyth's own models of the percussion lock he invented after years of experiment in the Tower. Superseding the flintlock, it completely revolutionised firearms development and, consequently, the science of war.

ACKNOWLEDGMENTS (in addition to those already made): The following Crown Copyright photographs are reproduced by permission of the Department of the Environment: pages 6, 15 (all three), 22, 23. The portraits except that of Henry VI and Princess Elizabeth p. 17 which are from the Royal Collection and reproduced by gracious permission of H.M. The Queen are from the National Portrait Gallery. Other photographs are by S. W. Newbery, Hon. F.I.I.P., F.R.P.S., Kenneth Scowen, F.I.I.P., F.R.P.S. and Reginald Davis, F.I.I.P., F.R.P.S.